MANIFESTOS FOR THE 21ST CENTURY

SERIES EDITORS: URSULA OWEN AND JUDITH VIDAL-HALL

Free expression is as high on the agenda as it has ever been, though not always for the happiest of reasons. Here, distinguished writers address the issue of censorship in a complex and fragile world where people with widely different cultural habits and beliefs are living in close proximity, where offence is easily taken, and where words, images and behaviour are coming under the closest scrutiny. These books will surprise, clarify and provoke in equal measure.

WHOSE LIBERTY IS IT ANYWAY?

Europe at the Crossroads

STEFAN AUER

WITH THE ASSISTANCE OF

NICOLE SCICLUNA

Seagull
BOOKS

LONDON NEW YORK CALCUTTA

Seagull Books, 2012

ISBN-13 978 0 8574 2 040 4

British Library Cataloguing-in-Publication Data
A catalogue record for this book is available
from the British Library

Typeset and designed by Seagull Books, Calcutta, India
Printed and bound by Hyam Entreprises, Calcutta

CONTENTS

ACKNOWLEDGEMENTS

For their generous support, assistance and feedback, I wish to thank Philip Bull, Simon Garnett, Kyra Giorgi, John Hirst, Matt Killingsworth, Gosia Klatt, Jan Pakulski, Robert Podbereski, Manfred Sapper, Luke Slattery, Danielle Vida and especially Judith Vidal-Hall. The research on this book was partly supported by a Discovery Grant from the Australian Research Council.

'European: one who is nostalgic for Europe,'[1] remarked Milan Kundera, elliptically, in the mid-1980s, decades before such gloomy diagnoses again became fashionable. Nostalgic for what? Europe's past greatness, of course. But does anyone today care to remember when and why it was so great? For writers and artists, Europe's greatness was its culture; for economists and more practically minded people, its tremendous wealth; for liberals, its commitment to liberty and the rule of law; for socialists, its devotion to equality and fairness; for dreamers, all of these.

Europe's better times were meant to be ahead of it. Not so long ago, the European dream was believed to have provided the best 'vision of the future'.[2] Europe was going to 'run the twenty-first century', as Mark Leonard argues,[3] having created 'an entirely new species of human organization, the likes of which the world has never seen'.[4] If the West—and most of the world—was American in the twentieth century, the twenty-first was going to be European. But not in any crude, old-fashioned, imperial, my-values-are-better-than-yours kind of way; rather, in an open and open-ended, reflexive, self-critical, you-are-as-good-as-or-better-than-me way. Europe was going to lead the world by example—but gently. 'Soft power Europe' would rule without anyone noticing but everyone benefitting. All these assumptions proved hubristic: Europe's turn of fortune is humbling, humiliating and, perhaps, irreversible.

As Europe was falling apart in 2010–12, even some of the more sceptical voices seemed too optimistic. Hans Magnus Enzensberger bemoaned the rise of the 'gentle monster Brussels' just as the European Union (EU) was forced to put aside its velvet gloves the better to preach the virtues of austerity, thus accelerating what Enzensberger termed 'the disenfranchisement of Europe'.[5] Legal scholars were concerned about the 'cumbersomeness of EU Law', before noticing that the EU's peculiar legal system would be resented as oppressive once it began to infringe on people's ideas of self-government. Self-declared pessimist Roger Scruton was vindicated by the EU's growing role at the heart of the rapidly deteriorating economic situation. While EU elites continued to preach the mantra of salvation through greater supranationalism, Scruton denounced the EU as 'the most far-reaching piece of institutionalized folly that the free world currently witnesses'.[6]

What went wrong, and when? Europe's most audacious moment occurred some time between 1989 and 1991, a short period that encapsulated both the demise of Communism in Central and Eastern Europe—from Poland, Hungary, East Germany and Czechoslovakia in 1989 to the Soviet Union in 1991—and the bold step forward on the path to an 'ever-closer union' in Western Europe. Twenty years later, the accomplishment of post-Second World War European unity proved extremely fragile and the significant failures of economic and political integration forced Europeans to reconsider the underpinnings of their project. Though it appeared in different shapes and sizes, and had numerous causes outside Europe (the US sub-prime crisis, for example), the economic crisis in 2010–12 also manifested itself as a crisis of European democracy. Old questions acquired new meaning: Is it possible to maintain conditions for self-government while undermining the nation-state? What are the limits of solidarity? Can Europe be truly united through its common history or its common currency? Do we even need more unity in Europe?

Whose Liberty is it Anyway? addresses these questions through two major strands. First, it shows how the EU failed in its attempt to forge a stronger sense of shared history by appropriating a variety of symbols and historical moments. The politics of memory applied to 1989, for example, clearly exposed the limitations of top-down identity-building. Second, it focuses on another flawed attempt at strengthening unity—the creation of a monetary union with a shared currency, the Euro. This is a project that, in many ways, arose out of the events of 1989–90—in particular, the perceived need to anchor a reunified Germany more firmly within Europe. A comparison between monetary as well as political union in Germany and Europe is both ironic and instructive: ironic, because one of the notable effects of the Eurozone crisis, which became more visible in 2010, has been Germany's rise to political as well as economic pre-eminence in Europe; instructive, because the smaller-scale, pragmatic and overwhelmingly successful process of German reunification highlights many of the flaws in the overly ambitious European attempts at monetary and political union.

Europe's radical transformation from a mere common market into a true political union had other significant aspects that feature less prominently here: the advent of European citizenship and the abortive Constitutional Treaty. EU citizenship, along with the Economic and Monetary Union, was first introduced by the Maastricht Treaty which came into effect in 1993. While its consequences do not prove to be as damaging as those of the common currency, the considerable differences between the rhetoric and the reality of supranational citizenship also expose the EU's limitations. These limitations were even more starkly revealed by the 2005 failure of the Constitutional Treaty designed to infuse Europeans with a renewed pro-integration ethos.

Each of these EU initiatives has backfired: the higher they aimed the greater their fall. Much more than a transnational medium of exchange, the common currency was intended to be the symbol of united Europe par excellence. Instead, the Eurozone crisis has reinforced latent suspicions, if not hostilities, between EU nations. Similarly, citizenship rights aimed at strengthening the internal market by facilitating mobility also became part of the EU's efforts to engender in ordinary people a sense of belonging to the Union. But the restrictions placed on the application for EU citizenship made some Europeans feel like second-class citizens. The EU's Constitutional Treaty also combined pragmatic reforms, meant to streamline institutions and decision-making processes, with heavy doses of political rhetoric and symbolism. Its failure to deliver these weakened the Union.

The EU and its leaders justified each of these initiatives via a deceptively pleasing narrative: the history of European integration is a story of peace, prosperity and progress. It is the story of the recovery and redemption of a war-torn continent. The events of 1989—the collapse of Communism and the subsequent reunification of East and West—fit seamlessly into this story. It is also dynamic and forward-looking: we must continue on the path of ever-closer union because the fate of Europe depends on it. Such an approach to history had to airbrush numerous contradictions and inconsistencies, as the events of 1989 and their later interpretation will illustrate. It also undermined the EU's real achievements and genuine potential, thereby seriously damaging the European project.

Despite, or rather, *because* of, its preoccupation with what the Constitutional Treaty calls 'forg[ing] a common destiny', the EU of the twenty-first century has lost its way.

1989: ONE YEAR, TWO TALES. CAN EUROPE BE UNITED BY A COMMON HISTORY?

The EU loves anniversaries. Emulating the earlier experiences of nation-states, it has resorted to some of the strategies that proved successful in creating nations: celebrating those events that mark the key moments in its history and even building a museum which, when it opens in Brussels in 2014, intends to serve as a lasting treasure trove of European memory. To shape its future, the EU seeks to control its past.

But Europe is far too diverse to be able to turn its many histories into one unifying narrative. From the outset, the European project was based on a somewhat paradoxical relationship with its past. Europeans were initially united more by what they rejected than by that to which they aspired. Paul Valéry's famous dictum from 1922 can also be used to describe the post-Second World War sentiment: 'We hope vaguely, we dread precisely.'[7] What people vaguely hoped for was peace; what they dreaded was the devastation of past wars. Back then, forgetting was perhaps more widespread—and may have been more conducive to peace—than remembering: 'Europeans took shelter behind a collective amnesia. Reality was not just ignored, it was flatly denied.'[8] Considering Europe's troublesome heritage, this is not surprising. As Polish philosopher Leszek Kołakowski reminds us:

> The history of Europe had its admirable episodes and its moments of glory, but they were only moments. It was European civilization that created the totalitarian ideologies of the

> twentieth century: Nazism, Communism, Fascism. These were not the crazed fantasies of a few fanatics but bold, powerful and well-organized mass movements with a strong ideological base. Communism was the degenerate bastard-child of the Enlightenment, Nazism the degenerate bastard-child of Romanticism.[9]

To find more positive sources of identification in their past, Europeans were better served by reaching further back to the best aspects of the Enlightenment: its cosmopolitan spirit, its Romanticism, its ideal of the European family of nations advanced in the nineteenth century by the likes of Victor Hugo in France[10] and Giuseppe Mazzini in Italy. Perhaps the best-known expression of the spirit of both the European Enlightenment and Romanticism is to be found in Beethoven's Ninth Symphony incorporating Schiller's 'Ode to Joy'. It is thus fitting that the EU adopted the tune of the symphony's finale as its anthem in 1986.

Celebrating freedom, Beethoven took the liberty of experimenting with a well-established musical form. In fact, for many musicologists, Beethoven's Ninth marks one of the most audacious moments in musical history: never before had a composer introduced a human voice into a symphony's finale. Beethoven's project was deemed 'an unrealizable one' but, alas, this would not deter the great composer: '"Must it be? It must be!" Yes it must be—because Beethoven wanted it to be!'[11] The enduring popularity of Beethoven's composition suggests that radical changes have a better chance of success in music than in European society, whether one thinks of the French Revolution of 1789 that influenced the composer profoundly or of the radical transformation of Europe after 1989 that is our focus here. Bold experiments in music might be worthwhile but in politics, as Edmund Burke understood better than anyone, experimentation often leads to disaster, for politics is the art of the possible. Recognizing one's limits is preferable to losing one's way in the pursuit of limitless possibilities.

In fact, one of the keys to understanding the European project's initial success was its limited ambition, both in its scope and its aims. Initially limited to six countries of Western Europe and underpinned by a strong commitment to liberal democracy, it aimed at securing peace and prosperity. 'Public protestations to the contrary notwithstanding,' noted Tony Judt, 'the European Community of the 1970s and 80s not only presumed the permanence of Europe's division but depended upon it.'[12] Furthermore, aside from the Community's rhetorical commitment to an ever-closer union made in the founding Treaty of Rome (1957), its aim was not a supranational project of the 'United States of

Europe'. On the contrary, the pragmatic realism of the post-Second World War political elites in Western Europe and their enlightened concern with national interests resulted in the European rescue of the nation-state, as Alan S. Milward argues in his seminal work.[13]

The collapse of Communism opened up new opportunities to reach beyond these limitations. For the first time in their turbulent histories, the nations of Europe in the West *and* in the East could pursue unity together. Thanks to the end of the Cold War divide, Europe was going to be ever bigger; thanks to its determination to unify further, it was going to be ever-more-deeply integrated. The peaceful revolutions in Central and Eastern Europe gave the European Union a new set of images and a date to remember: 9 November 1989, the day the Berlin Wall lost its purpose.

One of the first public celebrations of this event was the performance of Beethoven's Ninth by a multinational orchestra with musicians from Germany, Russia, UK, US and France, and conducted by Leonard Bernstein in the Schauspielhaus Berlin (East Germany). For this occasion, even Schiller's unforgettable poem needed editing. Responding to the spirit of the time—the concert took place only a few weeks after the demise of the Wall—Bernstein felt justified in making a small but significant change to Schiller's lyrics, substituting the word *Freiheit* (freedom) for *Freude* (joy). Ever since, the liberation of 1989 and Beethoven's famous finale seem to have gone hand in hand as positive symbols of European unity. The same music accompanied the celebrations of the 'Big Bang' enlargement in May 2004, which brought eight countries from the former Eastern bloc into the EU, followed by the admission of Bulgaria and Romania in January 2007.[14]

Twenty years after the demise of Communism, the EU has more than doubled in size, from the initial 6 members in 1957 to the 12 in 1989 to the current 27. Such a radical widening required institutional changes. Indeed, since the Maastricht Treaty in 1993, the EU has ratified three major reform treaties. The most recent of these, the 2009 Lisbon Treaty, is itself the culmination of a decade-long—and ultimately unsuccessful—bid to furnish the EU with a constitution. The reform process has been slow, painful and marked by compromise upon compromise, to the point that the treaties are rendered virtually unreadable and the governing structures incomprehensible.

However, as difficult as this process has been, treaty reform is only one dimension of the EU's post-Communism mission to reinvent itself. The 27-member-strong EU needs more than new institutions: it requires a new self-understanding. Judging from a number of attempts by key EU actors, achieving a consensus on the 'meaning' of decisive events in Europe's recent past is no less difficult than the protracted process of institutional reform.

FROM SCHUMAN TO MAASTRICHT: EUROPE DAY AND THE EUROPEAN ANTHEM

Since 1985, Eurocrats have had a day off every 9 May to celebrate the EU's official birthday, a commemoration of the Schuman Declaration. The Declaration of 9 May 1950 harked back to the legacy of the Second World War and aimed at the preservation of peace in Europe by means of piecemeal economic cooperation, which would 'create de facto solidarity'. French Foreign Minister Robert Schuman was fully aware of the significance of its timing, 'almost five years to the day since Germany's unconditional surrender', even though the actual release date of his plan was contingent on a series of negotiations between French, American and British partners. Jean Monnet, the architect of the Schuman Declaration, later recalled that, in order to overcome traditional enmities between France and Germany, 'the Franco-German problem' had to be turned into 'a European problem'. From a more sceptical perspective, 'the French were successful beyond their wildest hopes in "Europeanizing" their historical difficulty by incorporating West Germany into a Franco-centric community where France got what its leaders thought it needed without appearing to have done so by conventionally selfish means.'[15] France and Germany were soon joined in this endeavour by Italy and the Benelux countries—The Netherlands, Belgium and Luxembourg.

Whether it was driven by European idealism or French national interests, it is worthwhile to remember that the Schuman Declaration was *not* perceived as a major event with far-reaching consequences by many of its contemporaries. The fact that it is now considered a milestone in Europe's integration is largely a testimony to the success of the

European Commission and other EU institutions in making it so. But Europe Day is not, for a number of reasons, entirely appropriate as a symbol uniting *all* the peoples of Europe.

One, it is a reminder of the elitist and secretive nature of the project, at least originally when there was very little 'popular European feeling of community'.[16] To protect peace in Europe, its people had to be protected from themselves: from their fear and distrust of their neighbours, from their desire for revenge. Owing to such sentiments, a people's Europe had to be built largely without people's knowledge of it; even to this day, not many outside Brussels are aware of the Schuman Declaration. This did not pose any significant problems as long as the European project did not have much effect on the daily lives of citizens; but that began to change dramatically in the 1980s.

Two, 9 May is indelibly tainted by a historical trauma in Central and Eastern Europe.

Unlike in the West, where the end of the Second World War is commemorated on 8 May, people in the Soviet bloc were compelled to celebrate it a day later because Georgy Zhukov, Marshal of the Soviet Union, happened to arrive in Berlin later than the Allied leaders. The fundamental difference between 8 and 9 May is that the former denotes the liberation of Western Europe—including West Germany—while the latter reminds people of the ensuing expansion of the Soviet Empire. For Poland and the Baltic countries in particular, the date simply marks the replacement of one totalitarian regime, Nazism, with another, Stalinism.

If the Schuman Declaration, enshrined in Europe Day, can be seen as a practical answer to the prevalent *negative* sentiment in Europe immediately after the Second World War, the 'never-again war',[17] then the European anthem is the expression of the *positive* eighteenth-century ideal of the universal brotherhood of man. Both seek to foster European unity: the former through a shared sense of revulsion at a history marred by excessive violence; and the latter by reminding Europeans of their Enlightenment heritage as embodied in the ideals of the French Revolution (but not in its practice, since it too was not free from violence). European citizenship combines the pragmatic spirit of the Schuman Declaration with the cosmopolitan ideal expressed in the European anthem.[18] It is pragmatic in that it merely supplements, rather than substitutes, the existing national citizenship. Still, by reminding Europe's citizens of the rights they have as Europeans—freedom of movement, in particular—European citizenship aimed to enhance a sense of European identity. The downside was that those Europeans whose EU rights were constrained—such as the citizens in the new member states for almost a decade after the 2004 enlargement and most Roma, perhaps permanently—were made to feel inferior to their West European counterparts.

While Europe Day reminds some Europeans of Stalinist repression, even Beethoven's Ninth is not free from the demons of Europe's past. Beethoven's uplifting symphony was not only appropriated for bold, progressive, humanist projects but was also used by the Nazis to great effect in their propaganda. Joseph Goebbels, for instance, requested a performance of the symphony to celebrate Hitler's birthday in 1937. It is odd, then, that the European political elites could not think of anyone else when they commissioned the former Nazi Party member, Herbert von Karajan, to adapt Beethoven's music for the European anthem, ignoring 'the moral dissonance [which] the strange trilogy of Schiller–Beethoven–Karajan evokes'.[19]

Would 9 November 1989 offer a better symbol for European unity? The end of Communism took political elites in the West by surprise. Though the EU had contributed very little to the end of the Cold War and was slow to develop an adequate response to it, this did not prevent it from claiming responsibility for this unexpected change. To increase its credibility as a 'people's Europe', it was logical for the EU to appropriate the 'people's revolutions' of 1989.[20]

9 NOVEMBER 1989: LIBERTY AT LAST?

Having established an anthem and a Europe Day, the EU was suddenly presented with a new symbol capable of eliciting true affection: the fall of the Berlin Wall, along with images of people experiencing freedom. In May 2009, the European Commission Audiovisual Services released a three-minute video officially titled the 'Twentieth Anniversary of Democratic Change in Central and Eastern Europe'[21] to mark the occasion. Its story is as simple as it is captivating. Against the background of an extremely brief recapitulation of key moments in the struggle against Communism—Hungary, 1956; Czechoslovakia, 1968; Poland, 1981; Lithuania, Latvia, Estonia, 1989; Romania, 1989—the short film depicts a Europe without borders through the personal experience of someone born on that memorable day, 9 November 1989. The story is as follows. A boy is born at the very moment liberty is born in Berlin: liberty for Germany and the whole of Europe. Uplifting music underlines the young parents' joy over the newborn, reinforced through public joy over the fall of the Wall (as can be seen on a TV screen in the maternity ward). As the boy learns to walk, the countries of the former Eastern bloc take their first steps towards national independence and freedom (the withdrawal of Soviet troops from Hungary in June 1991, the independence of Lithuania in November 1991). When the boy turns six, the small family drives to France for a holiday, experiencing the newly established Europe without borders ('Open borders', 1995). Later, the boy, now 15, celebrates the enlargement of the European Union ('Europe reunited', 2004). Finally, taking a photograph of the Brandenburg Gate, the young adult is ambushed by friends who then join him to celebrate his twentieth birthday.

Although this sanitized, politically correct depiction of birthday celebrations aimed to please everyone (somewhat implausibly, 20-year-olds chose to celebrate with strawberry cake and soft drinks!), it triggered a minor upheaval in the Polish media and on the pages of YouTube. From the EU perspective, the storyline made perfect sense as a lively and visually engaging production that effectively assimilated the revolutions of 1989 into the established narrative of *West* European integration. It is surely not accidental that the young family chose France as its holiday destination. Rather, the choice reinforced the common understanding: that at the centre of the European project was the process of Franco-German reconciliation which turned both countries into reliable partners—for each other and for Europe at large. For a long time, France and Germany have been seen as the engine of European integration and, after the demise of Communism in Central and Eastern Europe, this model of reconciliation was expected to extend to the whole continent.

Yet, even as the film celebrated a Europe without borders—realized through the Schengen Agreement in 1995—citizens from Poland and other countries of Central and Eastern Europe had to accept restrictions on their freedom of movement: they could not work in Germany before 2011, for example, owing to a transitional measure that the old member states were allowed to apply to people from the new member states. France lifted its restrictions in July 2008, four years after the 2004 enlargement, having recovered from the somewhat paranoid fear of East European migrants undercutting French jobs. Famously embodied in the apocryphal 'Polish plumber', this combination of right-wing xenophobia and left-wing concern for labour and welfare standards was, in fact, a major contributing factor to the defeat of the Constitutional Treaty through the 2005 referendum in France.

From the Polish perspective, the timing of the video release could not have been worse. While the European Commission Audiovisual Services might have conceived it as a timely reminder of the fifth anniversary of the 2004 enlargement, Poles were about to celebrate the twentieth anniversary of their first semi-free elections on 4 June 1989. That key event in Polish history was largely overshadowed by more tragic and dramatic developments in China—the violent suppression of the pro-democracy movement in Tiananmen Square provided far more exciting media images—as well as by the EU video with its celebration of the fall of the Berlin Wall. As a number of Polish commentators and politicians observed, Poland's contribution was reduced, in the EU video, to a few seconds of footage of General Jaruzelski reading the martial law proclamation on 14 December 1981. There was no mention of Solidarność (Solidarity), of key personalities in the Polish struggle for liberty, such as John Paul II and Lech Wałęsa, nor any reference to the round-table discussions. Not surprisingly, Polish political elites across ideological divides, journalists and citizens were united in their rejection of the EU video.

Confronted with such a hostile reaction, the European Commission felt the need to respond and released an amended version that expanded the footage of the Polish contribution. It still failed to satisfy most Polish commentators. In addition, the European Commission Representation in Poland, in collaboration with the Office of the Committee for

European Integration, created a new video modelled on the original but with a distinctly different focus: Marta Włóka, a Polish student of Łódź University, who was born on 4 June 1989. It presented a day in her life alongside key moments in post-Communist Polish history, including the country's entry into the European Union. The final scene shows her saying a simple *dziękuję* (thank you), presumably, to all those who brought about a free Poland in a free Europe.[22]

The controversy about the EU representation of 1989 is not a trivial matter; from a Polish perspective the depiction of freedom without Solidarity is not just incomplete, it is offensive. Unwittingly, it also revives old traumas. It reminds Poles that, when it mattered, the rise and fall of the Solidarity movement was not met with sufficient solidarity by leading politicians in Western Europe, particularly in Germany. Similarly, in the immediate aftermath of the demise of Communism in Central and Eastern Europe, West Europeans—with the notable exception of UK Prime Minister Margaret Thatcher—were preoccupied with *West* European integration and the unification of Germany rather than with the enlargement of the European Union.

To understand the intensity of Polish responses to the 'Twentieth Anniversary' video, it is important to bear in mind that this was not just an isolated case. Two more examples show a broader pattern of biased representations of history that offended Polish sensitivities. While the publication of Franco-German history textbooks for secondary schools (*Histoire/Geschichte*: *L'Europe et le monde depuis 1945/Europa und die Welt seit 1945*; History/History: Europe and the World since 1945) in 2006 may have contributed to the reconciliation between France and Germany, it was done at the expense of serious distortions of other European countries, including Poland. As Polish historian and Member of the European Parliament (MEP) Wojciech Roszkowski argues in a detailed study, among the major omissions in the book is its failure to mention the Soviet invasion of Poland on 17 September 1939 and, once again, the contribution of Solidarity. One does not need to accept all of Roszkowski's harsh criticisms to acknowledge the shortcomings of an account of European history that focuses excessively on France and Germany.[23]

But perhaps the boldest and most widely controversial step so far in the EU's attempts to shape its history in its own image is the establishment of the House of European History, set to open in Brussels in 2014. Proposed by the then president of the European Parliament, Dr Hans-Gert Pöttering, it began with a carefully designed plan that was meant to please everyone and, perhaps not surprisingly, offended so many national sensitivities that further planning occurred virtually in secret. The agreed 'conceptual basis for a

House of European History' prompted official protests from numerous MEPs, mainly from the new member states, who were concerned about 'a number of serious omissions and misinterpretations'.[24] Another source of concern was the significant costs incurred at a time of severe budgetary crisis in almost every member state. Even people sympathetic to the idea of a Europe-wide politics of memory were disappointed that the EU had missed an opportunity to instigate an open debate on the meaning of its many histories.[25]

13 DECEMBER 1981: NOT ENOUGH SOLIDARITY WITH WORKERS' SOLIDARITY

Successive West German governments before 1989 had to deal with a fundamental dilemma in the Polish–German relationship: How to bring about a process of genuine reconciliation with a nation that was not ruled by a legitimate government? Official gestures of friendship and humility prevalent under the

Social Democratic strategy of Ostpolitik—aimed at defusing tensions between East and West, including between Poland and West Germany—unwittingly strengthened the legitimacy of the Communist rulers. Even the most memorable image of Ostpolitik, Willy Brandt's *Kniefall* [*von Warschau*] in front of the Monument to the Ghetto Heroes in Warsaw in December 1970, was not free of such entanglements. In the view of many Poles, it occurred in 'the wrong place at the wrong time',[26] particularly because the gesture could not be protected from the uses and abuses of Polish Communist propaganda.

One of the key aims of Ostpolitik was to improve the relationship between East and West Germany in order to ease the predicament of many Germans affected by the division. Implicitly, this strategy was based on the understanding that the division of Europe could not be changed in the foreseeable future. Helmut Schmidt sought to build on the legacy of Brandt's policies towards the East. In one of the most difficult moments of his political career, he found himself visiting East Germany on 13 December 1981, the day on which General Jaruzelski proclaimed martial law, yet another 'wrong place at the wrong time' in the Polish–German relationship. Schmidt was unwilling to jeopardize the progress made in the German–German relationship, even if this required a more muted response to the events in Poland. Queried by West German journalists about the events in Poland, he ended up agreeing with his host Erich Honecker, the leader of the East German state, that Jaruzelski's radical step was necessary to preserve peace and political stability in Europe. Schmidt continued to praise the visit as a sign of a 'good neighbourly relationship' and therefore attracted fierce criticisms from the right-of-centre media.[27] The editorials in *Der Spiegel*, the major left-wing weekly, shared Schmidt's concern with political instability, dismissing 'Polish romantic dreams of greatness'[28] and blaming the Solidarity movement for endangering peace in Europe. Similar arguments were also advanced by Brandt in his new role as the leader of the Socialist International.[29]

Schmidt's dilemma epitomized the serious difficulties faced by left-wing politicians in Western Europe more generally in their attitudes towards Central and Eastern Europe. While many were clearly sympathetic towards the first genuinely independent trade union in the Eastern bloc, they resented the anti-Communist elements in Poland and among Solidarity's supporters in the West. Major left-wing parties in the West (in France and Italy, for example) were hence divided about the appropriate response to the crises in Poland. This echoed earlier divisions about the appropriate attitude towards dissident intellectuals in Czechoslovakia grouped round Václav Havel's Charter 77 movement. While the US administration led by Jimmy Carter was proactive in advocating more political freedom throughout the Communist bloc, the West German government and a number of intellectuals in Western Europe were concerned that such 'human-rights diplomacy' would jeopardize Europe's political stability. The policy of detente was seen as more responsible and realistic than Carter's 'crusade for human rights'. In contrast, Havel's seminal essay of 1985, 'Anatomy of a Reticence',[30] spoke for many a dissident distrustful of the Western peace movement which unwittingly supported Soviet domination in Central and Eastern Europe.

9 NOVEMBER 1989: TOWARDS A 'EUROPEAN GERMANY' OR A 'FRANCO-GERMAN EUROPE'?

In another twist of history, the German–German relationship interfered with the German–Polish relationship on 9 November 1989. Just at the time of the fall of the Wall, the then German chancellor Helmut Kohl was visiting Poland. Confronted with the rapidly changing political situation in East Germany, Kohl felt that he had no option but to interrupt his official visit and fly back home. As Kohl noted in his memoirs, the historical significance of the event was highlighted by the Bundestag spontaneously intoning the German national anthem. This was a symbolically pregnant gesture that marked a departure from an unwritten consensus in West Germany on the postwar Federal Republic (Bonner Republik) as a 'post-national' construct. The fact that the opening stanza of the anthem is about a Germany that is to be free and united was immensely fitting to the occasion.[31]

Kohl also recalled that his Polish hosts were understandably displeased about the interruption of the trip, particularly against the background of the 'growing awareness that they were witnessing a development at the end of which Poland would find itself next to a reunified Germany with a population of 80 million'.[32] Many Poles, alongside people in France and UK, as well as a number of intellectuals and politicians in both East and West Germany, were chary about the emergence of a powerful Germany that might destabilize Europe.

Given the traumatic history of the Polish–German relationship, it is not surprising that a large proportion of Poles were against German reunification: 36.5 per cent according to a snapshot survey published in *Gazeta Wyborcza* on 10 November 1989. If anything, it is remarkable that so many, almost 40 per cent according to the same survey, were in favour of it.[33] This might partly be explained by the fact that Polish dissidents were well prepared conceptually for this situation, having contemplated the possibility of German reunification long before it was considered a realistic proposition even in Germany itself.

As early as 1977, Polskie Porozumienie Niepodległościowe, the so-called Polish Alliance for Independence, argued that Polish aspirations for liberty must go hand in hand with the acceptance of the eventual unification of Germany. In a 1978 document published in *Kultura*, an influential Polish exile monthly, the Alliance explicitly argued that 'German unification is in Poland's interest, provided two conditions are fulfilled: the unconditional recognition of our western border; and that Germany would be fully integrated into the European Community.'[34]

The largely pro-German sentiment from within the Solidarity had increased the temptation to forget about the traditional anti-German sentiment in Poland. It therefore came as a surprise to West European leaders when the more nationalist Polish government led by the Kaczyński twins [Lech and Jarosław] transformed these xenophobic sentiments into programmatic politics. The low point was a dispute about the voting rights in the EU Council that escalated in June 2007 when Jarosław Kaczyński argued for the preservation of the disproportional weighting in Poland's favour on the basis that, 'If Poland had not had to live through the years of 1939–45, Poland would today be looking at the demographics of a country of 66 million.'[35] Such remarks broke a well-established taboo: EU elites were not accustomed to openly voicing accusations going back to the Second World War, despite the obvious fact that its legacy had shaped the EU decisively.

It was against this historical background that the EU communication strategy on the 'meaning of 1989' was bound to backfire. In contrast to the European Commission and its Audiovisual Services, German politicians have demonstrated a greater awareness of their past shortcomings and misjudgements vis-à-vis Poland. Gerhard Schröder, for example, came close to apologizing for those aspects of

Ostpolitik that appeared to have led to his predecessors siding with the Polish Communist government rather than with the Polish people. In a speech delivered in December 2000 to a joint session of the Polish parliament and senate, Schröder acknowledged that to the extent to which 'a number of German politicians, including some Social Democrats, prioritized stability at the time of the rise of Solidarity, they failed to do justice to the historic significance of the Polish fight for liberty'.[36] Echoing this sentiment, the leading editorial in the *Frankfurter Allgemeine Zeitung* on 4 June 2009, 20 years after the first semi-free elections in Poland, stressed the importance of Poland as 'the first domino' that led to the eventual fall of Communism in Europe. On the same day, German Chancellor Angela Merkel, attending the commemoration of the elections in Warsaw, thanked Poles for their contribution to liberty in Europe with a simple '*dziękuję bardzo* (many thanks), for ever'.

Symbolic politics—missteps in EU attempts to appropriate the meaning of 1989 notwithstanding—have contributed to the process of Polish–German reconciliation. When Poland assumed the EU presidency in July 2011, it did so from a position of confidence, assured of its place in Europe both politically and economically. Ironically, it advocated more integration and transnational European solidarity just after it had demonstrated the advantages of staying outside one of the key projects of European unity—the Eurozone. Poland is one of the few countries in the West that did not experience a recession as a result of the global financial crisis, largely because it has not yet entered the common currency. This has afforded it some flexibility in responding to external pressures.

At any rate, in 2010–12, 'the crisis of the Eurozone overshadowed the crisis of European memory.'[37] Conflicting material interests appeared more important than conflicts about history. If anything, disputes about appropriate action in response to deteriorating economic conditions were, at times, aggravated by crude accusations against Germany that the process of European unification had been intended to overcome: a number of commentators critical of German leadership of the Eurozone rescue efforts invoked painful memories of German domination during the Second World War. This was the opposite of what the common currency was meant to achieve.

CAN EUROPE BE UNITED BY A COMMON CURRENCY?

The creation of the Economic and Monetary Union in 1992 cannot be separated from the dramatic events of 1989–90. The prospect of a populous and powerful reunified Germany at the heart of Europe led Germany's European partners, particularly France, to seek ways of embedding that country more securely in Europe. This was one of the key rationales behind the common currency. In return for giving up their beloved Deutschmark, one of the great symbols of postwar West German recovery, the Germans would gain the trust of their European partners and support for the speedy reunification of their country.

Other concessions were made to German sensibilities. The new Euro would be as strong and stable as the Deutschmark with an independent European Central Bank (ECB), based in Frankfurt, committed to maintaining low inflation. However, as the sovereign debt crisis spread through Europe in 2010–12, it was clear that neither the currency nor the ECB had lived up to these promises. The seeds of the Eurozone's current woes were sown much earlier, both in the repeated violation of the Maastricht Treaty criteria (by several countries, including Germany) and, more fundamentally, in the very attempt to achieve monetary convergence between 17 vastly different economies.

Yet the unwavering commitment of EU elites to the official narrative of ever-closer union has prevented them from honestly acknowledging past mistakes and openly assessing the full range of possible solutions. Just as every positive event in postwar Europe must be linked to the EU, any problem in the integration project can only be countered by further integration. Only the EU can guide Europeans along the 'path of civilization, progress and prosperity', according to the preamble to the Constitutional Treaty. Without the Eurozone, 'then forget Europe; we're back to the balance of power politics of previous centuries.'[38]

GERMAN AND EUROPEAN UNIFICATION: TWO SIDES OF THE SAME COIN?

The building of a European quasi-state, with a common set of symbols and a common currency, is as misguided as the forging of German unity after 1989 was prudent. The two processes were closely interrelated and there are lessons to be drawn from one process about the other. German reunification on 3 October 1990 was faster than anyone could have anticipated. This was to a great degree the result of astute political leadership in West Germany, particularly by Chancellor Kohl, who was receptive to popular feelings among the East German people and their overwhelming desire for speedy unification, all the while managing concerns among its Western allies as well as its former Cold War foes in the East about the possible rebirth of an all-too-powerful Germany. The only significant political leader in the West opposed to this strategy was Thatcher, who was profoundly suspicious of both greater Germany and greater European unity—even though she was in favour of speedy enlargement—anticipating that this would undermine Europe's federalist agenda.

The success of German unification was predicated on the pragmatic approach of its key architects, who understood and accepted the political constraints of the time. Ambitious goals were pursued by moderate means. Kohl and his allies built on past achievements, inherited institutions and practices, rather than embarking on new experiments as desired by his political opponents in both West and East Germany. To make German unity work, it was vital to make full use of the crucial West German accomplishments: the Basic Law that underpinned the stability of its political system; and the Deutschmark that was both an expression and the precondition of its economic success. Internationally, existing structures such as NATO and the European Community were utilized rather than any radically new design such as the Common European House, advocated initially by Soviet leader Mikhail Gorbachev, or similar alternatives advanced by a number of dissident intellectuals such as Ulrike Poppe in East Germany or Václav Havel in Czechoslovakia.

However, while Kohl managed to sideline all attempts at new departures in East Germany—whether the 'Third Way', 'Real Socialism' or a neutral reunified Germany with a new purpose and a new constitution—he accepted and actively supported a radically new departure for the project of European unity. German unification after the fall of the Berlin Wall simply promised more of the same: the postwar Federal Republic, built on an adherence to fiscal discipline and the rule of law, simply extended further East. Europe, by contrast, was to change much more dramatically by living up to the initial promise of the Treaty of Rome for an ever-closer union among its peoples. It was to seize the opportunity provided by the collapse of Communism to recalibrate its mission and take the

European enterprise far beyond a common market.

Though people in East Germany may still be waiting for their former country to be turned into the 'flourishing landscapes' promised by Kohl at the height of unification euphoria, German unity has been accomplished. The process was not easy, and the costs were significant. And, more than 20 years later, West Germans still only grudgingly accept the so-called *Solidaritätszuschlag*, the special-purpose tax that enabled the German federal government to raise hundreds of billions of Euros in solidarity payments for the new federal states in the East. However, although it has been severely tested by the unification process, German national solidarity has survived.

1991, with 'Third Way' Communist Yugoslavia descending into civil war shortly after), Europe regained its determination to expand. Perhaps more significantly, the newly post-Communist states outside the Union strengthened their resolve to join. At the same time that a significant enlargement of Union membership was being contemplated, the EU radically shored up its commitment to further political and economic integration. The bigger the potential widening of the EU, the greater the accompanying deepening would need to be—or so went the prevalent argument.

German policies on reunification in 1989–90 echoed the cautious pragmatism of the founding fathers of European unity in 1950–57. On the other hand, Franco-German policies towards Europe in 1989–93 were reminiscent of the relentless optimism of the French revolutionaries of two centuries before. Why not turn Europe into a supranational state in which nations no longer worry about their sovereignty and in which people, European citizens, can move freely between its various countries? To facilitate this further, most, if not all, Europeans would use one common currency and enjoy the right of free movement without a passport. This was far too ambitious and occurred without popular demand. 'Must it be? It must be!' Yes it must be—because the European elites wanted it to be!

The French Revolution of 1789 succeeded, at least theoretically, in transferring sovereignty from the king to the citizens and the source of all political power and legitimacy from God to the nation. It was imagined that the Maastricht Treaty 'revolution' of 1993 could successfully push this project of universal emancipation further by weakening the link between democracy and the nation-state. At long last, thought EU enthusiasts, a post-national Europe seemed ready for 'constitutional patriotism', as Jürgen Habermas puts it,[39] and a truly 'cosmopolitan democracy' in Ulrich Beck's words.[40] In practice, the construct of European citizenship introduced by the Maastricht Treaty was less comprehensive than the proponents of a federalist United States of Europe might have wished; it was still derived from national citizenship and the political rights it endowed on people were limited. But the consequences of the Schengen Agreement, signed in 1985 and implemented a decade later, and the Maastricht Treaty, with their extensive provisions for freedom of movement, were profound: they had the potential to dramatically transform European societies.

THE EURO IN CRISIS: IS THIS THE END?

Merely a decade after its introduction, when a number of distinguished scholars and leading politicians were celebrating the success of the Euro, Europe was hit by the most severe economic crisis in its postwar history, one that exposed the fundamental weakness of the Eurozone. For EU federalists, this was no reason to doubt any of their projects; on the contrary: 'In the wake of 1989, are we today, in

2009, experiencing the second world revolution?' asked Beck with a great deal of enthusiasm tinged with trepidation. 'My God, what an opportunity!' he wrote, arguing:

> Who, if not the EU, has the necessary experience to invoke a supranational common good? [. . .] *If the EU did not exist, we would have to invent it today.* Far from being a threat to national sovereignty at the beginning of the 21st century, the EU first makes it possible [. . .] The pooled sovereignty of the EU provides the only hope for every nation and every citizen to live in freedom and peace [emphasis added].[41]

Beck strongly advocated even more political and economic integration, averring that 'the choice is between more Europe and no Europe'. This argument has been echoed by other leading German intellectuals such as Jürgen Habermas and Joschka Fischer, and by EU leaders such as José Manuel Barroso, Jean-Claude Trichet and Herman Van Rompuy. After some initial delay, national leaders followed suit. In August 2011, German Chancellor Angela Merkel and French President Nicholas Sarkozy called for an economic government for Europe, at least for the 17 countries of the Eurozone. With the notable exception of UK Prime Minister David Cameron, the only strategy that most leaders appeared to be willing to contemplate was moving towards a supranational Europe. This would entail not just a common currency but also harmonized taxation and a quasi-government, at least for economic matters. What these plans ignored was the lack of public support for measures that would further erode national sovereignty. Control over the national budget is perhaps one of the oldest prerogatives of all democratic governments. After all, the slogan that inspired the establishment of both British and American democracy was 'no taxation without representation'.

The ideal of pooling sovereignty might have its appeal in good times but, when nations are faced with the seemingly inescapable prospect of managing decline, this vision is reckless, almost dangerous. Even in Germany, ordinary citizens are opposed to a 'post-national Europe'. People at Europe's peripheries tend to find it even less attractive, fearing that the idea of European federation is a mere cover for German domination. Perhaps the most disturbing image employed by Greek demonstrators protesting against further austerity measures in 2011 was the EU flag with a swastika splashed across the centre. Though such images were not widespread, anti-German rhetoric across Europe became much more common than when Kaczyński first broke with the post-Second World War consensus of never mentioning the war in the high-stakes reform treaty negotiations in 2007.[42] At the height of the negotiations leading to the first rescue package in 2010, Greek Deputy Prime Minister Theodoros Pangalos was quoted as saying that 'the offspring of Nazis had no right to issue orders to Greeks.'[43] The popular Greek composer Mikis Theodorakis complained that 'the Greeks were becoming foreigners in their own country. This didn't happen even under the Nazi occupation.'[44]

UNINTENDED CONSEQUENCES

One of the unintended consequences of the common European currency is that it has strengthened nationalist sentiments by confirming national stereotypes. Germany withstood the pressures of the global financial crisis better than many other European nations thanks to its prudence and fiscal restraint, as did some northern European countries such as Finland, Sweden, the Netherlands and Denmark. Greece, Ireland, Italy,

Portugal and Spain were ill prepared for the crisis; neither efficiency nor money figured high on most people's national priorities. Their sceptical view of Germany will be reinforced through rising tensions caused by the conflicting strategies advocated for the rescue of the Eurozone.

The morality tale—those nations that were reckless and lived beyond their means should patiently endure the painful consequences, and those that were more prudent and thrifty should serve as a model to them—is difficult to accept even at the individual level; at the level of nations, that logic becomes grotesque. Clearly, not every Greek, Irish or Portuguese lived beyond their means.

The Germans are not indifferent to the views of others. The flagship organization for German culture and language, the Goethe-Institut, recently conducted a survey across 18 countries to establish what the people of Europe thought about Germany. Alongside an admiration for the German language, Europeans praised the German 'respect for rules' (Italians), 'order' (Hungarians, Poles), 'talent for organization' (Greeks, Portuguese and Spaniards), 'punctuality and diligence' (Slovaks). It goes without saying that these same people might not necessarily want to live in line with these virtues.[45] In fact, what was most disliked about the Germans was arguably not all that distant from the qualities they respected: their 'aloofness, arrogance' (Slovaks) and their 'lack of spontaneity' (Poles). Even the Germans sometimes complain about Germans in similar terms. Hans Ulrich Gumbrecht, one of the most astute observers of German culture and society and a professor of literature at Stanford University, also expressed his exasperation with the 'German *Rechthaberei*' (know-it-all attitude).[46]

How are such nationalist cliches relevant to the Eurozone? What the current crisis has brought into stark relief is the fact that a currency is always more than just a technical instrument. As Dutch writer Leon de Winter mused in 2010 while calling for the reintroduction of national currencies: 'The French used to have their elegant Franc that had the flair of an overcrowded Brasserie in Paris, and the Italians their Lira, that was as slutty and seductive as [Marcello] Mastroianni and [Anita] Ekberg in [Federico] Fellini's *La dolce vita*.'[47] To be sure, the Lira might have been more popular with tourists than with the Italians themselves, particularly after devaluation, but the Italians could live with it. They were not traumatized by endless zeros on their banknotes, and they could live with their unreliable currency as happily as with their chaotic political system.

The Germans are different. In the German public imagination, the trauma of inflation is firmly linked with the rise of Nazi Germany. There is probably no other country on earth where people see low inflation as their constitutional right. In mid-2011, the Federal Constitutional Court of Germany considered claims that the Eurozone rescue efforts undermined fundamental rights enshrined in the German Basic Law, including the right to property, which, so the claimants believed, would be compromised if the Eurozone rescue efforts proved inflationary.

The creation of the German currency union in mid-1990 spearheaded Germany's political unification in October of the same year. The creation of the common European currency a decade later, by contrast, threatens to destroy European unity by reinforcing latent animosities between its constituent nations.

In 2010–11, even German public opinion began to turn decisively against Europe. The fact that German and European interests were in harmony for the best part of the second half of the twentieth century makes that reversal even more significant. As Ulrike Guérot and Mark Leonard observed: 'Whereas Germans once saw the EU as the embodiment of postwar German virtues such as fiscal rectitude, stability and consensus, they now see it as a threat to those same virtues. Whereas many Europeans want Germany to save Europe, many Germans now want to be saved *from* Europe.'[48]

The Eurozone crisis has undermined the core values underpinning the contemporary German political system. The success of postwar West German democracy was predicated on two key commitments: West Germany's *raison d'être* was to be a 'good European' and to show its commitment to the *Rechtsstaat,* the rule of law. Until recently, all these goals went hand in hand. Germany has proven to be a reliable partner in a EU that succeeded precisely because it functioned as a rule-based supranational polity. The crisis has changed these basic parameters. The strategies employed to preserve the Eurozone are not free from bending the adopted rules, such as the no-bail-out clause in the Maastricht Treaty. Similarly, the independence of the ECB has been compromised. Germany's commitment to rules appears to be on a collision course with its commitment to Europe. The political elites in Germany and Europe sought to downplay this tension by talking about the need for more transnational solidarity.

But solidarity has its limits. For the principle of solidarity to work in a democratic polity, people must feel that their contributions will be directed to where they are most needed. To ensure that, they need a transparent and efficient public administration supported by a highly developed civic spirit. These are more easily found in some places than in others. Ideally, one would have the social capital of Sweden combined with the efficiency of German bureaucracy. But Greece is neither Sweden nor Germany, and no amount of supranational European governance will turn the Greek people into Protestant-work-ethic Swedes who love to pay taxes and respect their state institutions. They have had and continue to have good reasons to mistrust the state.

Yet there are limits to national cliches. Even Germans these days are not as thrifty as they may appear to Southern Europeans. It is a reflection of the dire state of public finances in Europe that Germany's economy, with a public debt higher than 80 per cent of its GDP, is considered to be 'healthy'. Paradoxically, one of the best performers in the Eurozone, in terms of its macroeconomic results and its relatively low level of sovereign debt—just above 40 per cent in 2010—is Slovakia, a country not known for high levels of social capital or trust in state institutions. Through trial and error, the Slovaks were able to create an economic and political model that suits their country. At the heart of it is a low flat tax of 19 per cent for all economic actors, including individual employees. It is besides the point here whether the system is fair or deficient; it was created through a democratic process, however messy, and is therefore seen as legitimate.

What the Slovaks do find difficult to accept is the necessity of contributing financially to the Eurozone rescue efforts. From their perspective, talk of pan-European solidarity sounds hollow when one of the poorest nations in the Eurozone is asked to help bail out one of the richest. The Slovak taxpayers, with one of the lowest average incomes in the Eurozone, are asked to subsidize the Irish, whose average income is still higher than the Germans. And with one of the least generous welfare states, they are asked to subsidize the overblown Greek state. In August 2010, the newly elected Slovak government reversed the previously adopted policy in support of the first Greek bail-out and Finance Minister Ivan Mikloš justified that position declaring:

'I do not consider it solidarity if it is solidarity between the poor and the rich, of the responsible with the irresponsible, or of taxpayers with bank owners and managers.'[49]

Regrettably, just a year later, Mikloš had to abandon his principled stand, accepting demands from his EU partners to increase the Slovak contribution to the Eurozone rescue effort. As this policy was blocked by Sloboda a Solidarita (Freedom and Solidarity), the minor coalition partner led by Richard Sulik, the government tried to secure parliamentary approval by combining the vote on the Eurozone contribution with a vote of confidence, which led to its collapse in October 2011. Defying the pressure from Germany as well as his coalition partners, Sulik had enough courage to state the obvious: the strategies pursued at the expense of taxpayers in the few countries that were still solvent were indefensible. Before losing his post as the speaker of the parliament and bringing down the government, Sulik said that he would rather be seen as an oddball by Brussels than be ashamed in front of his children for incurring on them unsustainable debts.[50] Predictably, his principled stance was rejected as populist posturing in the mainstream Slovak media, which felt a stronger allegiance towards European integration than the interests of the Slovak electorate. Sulik spoke fluent German, having spent 12 years as a young student in Munich, which helped in turning him into a prominent media personality in Germany too, if only for a few days.

This was not the first demise of a EU member-state government triggered by the Eurozone crisis. Early elections took place in 2011 in countries whose public debt had reached unsustainable levels, such as Ireland, Portugal and Spain. However, Slovakia was the first country in the EU whose government collapsed without any domestic economic problems. The erosion of democracy in Europe took a new turn for the worse in November 2011 when democratically elected governments in Greece and Italy succumbed to external pressure and were replaced by apolitical administrations. Increasingly, European political elites have sought to deal with the crisis by relying on technocratic leadership rather than on popular legitimacy.

These recent experiences undermine a concept in EU scholarship that is as trendy as it is fallacious: *demoicracy*. According to Kalypso Nicolaïdis: '[The EU] established itself as a new kind of political community, one defined not by a uniform identity—a *demos*—but by the persistent plurality of its peoples, its *demoi*. The EU is neither a union of democracies nor a union as democracy; it can now be a union of states and of peoples—a "*demoicracy*"—in the making.'[51]

Although the system of EU governance defies easy characterization, *demoicracy* obfuscates rather than illuminates its real nature.

Particularly problematic is the assumption that this novel arrangement would almost automatically lead to increased solidarity among European states and its peoples. Nicolaïdis argues that more sharing, mutual exchange and engagement creates a more integrated Europe. 'The glue that binds the EU together,' she writes, 'is not a shared identity; it is, rather, shared projects and objectives.'[52] However, what this account ignores is the possibility that shared projects might lead to greater mutual mistrust and hostility, particularly if they go awry, as has been the case with the common currency.

In a redistributive *demoicracy*, nations can be reduced to the status of a welfare recipient deprived of their basic liberties. The (supranational) state will provide for them, as long as they obey. The absurdity of this logic was on full display when Chancellor Merkel urged Greek people, after more than a year of austerity measures that showed no signs of delivering desired results, to try harder still: work longer hours and extend the average retirement age. The fact that her comment proved factually incorrect—at least, according to available statistics, Greek holiday entitlements were less generous than those in Germany—is less significant than its unsuitable, patronizing tone. Similar outrage was caused by comments made by the leader of the Eurozone group, Luxembourg Prime Minister Jean-Claude Juncker. In an interview with a German weekly, *Focus*, in July 2011 he stated bluntly that 'the sovereignty of Greece will be massively reduced'.[53] He was, of course, right, which made it all the worse. If any evidence was needed that the Greek people would have only a limited control over their destiny as long as they stayed within the Eurozone, it was delivered in early November 2011 when the then Prime Minister George Papandreou was forced to abandon his plan for a referendum about the proposed austerity measures.

Endless official references to the need for more transnational solidarity notwithstanding, what characterized the interdependence between the nations of the Eurozone 'was not freely exchanged solidarity but growing resentment and recrimination'.[54] This verdict from one of the most knowledgeable experts on the Euro, David Marsh, was devastating. The whole project was based on 'a gargantuan misunderstanding of the laws of economics'.[55] Marsh was not alone in predicting the difficulties of the common European currency; its demise has been dubbed the most widely predicted catastrophe and is going to be the more painful the longer it is delayed. And as Marsh points out, so much was expected from it:

> It would ban strife; promote social progress; control the Germans; increase growth, trade, wealth, investment and employment; quell inflation; counter the pre-eminence of

> the dollar; and buoy Europe's standing in the world. Never before had a new currency been so replete with anticipation, so desirous of achievement in so many fields; it was almost inevitable that, under the weight of these expectations, it would buckle.[56]

The problematic nature of costly Eurozone rescue efforts was magnified by their slim chances of success. Unwilling to accept the failure of their policies, in 2010–11 European political elites were pushing ahead with solutions that were bound to exacerbate the situation.

Comprehending the EU's problems requires a stretch of the imagination. How should one conceive, for example, of the total sum that the special-rescue mechanism, established in May 2010, was meant to make available, or the totality of all guarantees that the German government has made so far, rendering its electorate potentially liable to make payments worth hundreds of billions? The rescue facility for the Eurozone states that was created by the EU and the International Monetary Fund amounted initially to €750 billion, more than eight times the 2010 equivalent of the Marshall Plan aid to Europe after the Second World War, or more than twice the amount that was demanded from Germany in reparations after the First World War. The very fact that one has to consider examples from such distant European historical experience is disconcerting. Yet the Eurozone is *not* a new Versailles imposed on Germany, even if the liabilities were eventually to be turned into real payments. In the first place, the Eurozone was not imposed on Germany; even if the people did not welcome it, the German elites willingly endorsed it. And in the second, the German economy gained significant advantages from the common currency that seem to outweigh the costs (at least, at the time of writing in 2011).

Paradoxically, the spectre of the new Versailles applied better to Greece, as a leading German business paper, *Handelsblatt*, argued in November 2010. Its argument was as simple as it was compelling: you do not help a country in trouble by imposing punishing conditions on it.

Yet it is the unfortunate, if unintended, consequence of the common currency that Germany, as the most substantial benefactor, is compelled to assume the major responsibility for Greek public finances. To restore Greek control over its destiny, the Greek state might need to restore its national currency, as painful and messy as this step might be. At the time this manuscript went to press, both Greece and Italy were no longer ruled by democratically elected governments but, rather, technocratic leaders who took their orders from Berlin, Brussels and Frankfurt.

All the crucial steps on the common European currency were taken by France and

Germany, just as all significant attempts at Europe-wide identity-building were Franco-German initiatives. Just as most attempts at producing a unifying Franco-German story of Europe were resented by other nations, the attempt to create a European economic government advocated by France and Germany is unlikely to gain sufficient support from all 17 member states of the Eurozone, let alone the 27 EU member states.

Whatever strategy the Europeans end up adopting, their common currency will be transformed (provided it continues to exist). One way of describing competing scenarios is to resort yet again to national stereotypes. Initially, the Euro was meant to be as sound, dependable and reliable as the Deutschmark. German voters were promised that the ECB, like its spiritual predecessor, the German Bundesbank, was going to be governed by the same rules that made the Deutschmark so successful: complete independence from political pressures and a firm commitment to keeping inflation low. To ensure this, monetary policies (the central bank's domain) must also be separate from fiscal policies (the governments' domain). Though member-state governments were going to remain in charge of fiscal policies, they accepted contractual obligations, through the Maastricht Treaty, to follow strict rules: no more than 3 per cent budget deficit in any given year and no more than 60 per cent debt; and—one more promise to pacify German voters—no bail-outs.

For the first 5 to 10 years, the Euro was somewhat German in character. Inflation was low and, though the basic rules were occasionally violated, even by Germany and France, the regulatory framework remained reasonably solid and the ECB kept its independence and credibility. Around 2011, the Euro morphed into a French currency, not just because the ECB was headed by a Frenchman, Trichet, but also because of the unconventional policies pursued by the bank. By purchasing Greek, Italian and Spanish government bonds in secondary markets, the ECB compromised its political independence and undermined its credibility. One could call it a typically 'French solution'; with their statist political culture, French people are not strongly opposed to political interference in monetary policies.

By the time this book reaches its readers, the Euro may well have assumed a more Italian character and become more inflationary. It would be the last ironic twist in this unfolding drama: Mario Draghi, president of the ECB, who took office in November 2011, presented himself to German voters (and was praised by many commentators in Germany) as an Italian banker with unashamedly German virtues who would give priority to price stability, in other words, low inflation. However, when Greece defaults on its debt, as it will sooner or later, the ECB will be forced to write off significant losses. These losses will either have to be replenished by massive transfers of money from other member states, including Germany, or the ECB will simply print more money ('quantitative easing'). Whatever strategy is eventually adopted, the solution will make most European nations profoundly unhappy.

FUTURE SHOCK: DREAM OR NIGHTMARE?

The EU risks becoming a victim of its imagined success. Having moved well and truly beyond the common market created by the Treaty of Rome in 1957, a number of its more ambitious projects are now unravelling.

The attempt to build a European supranational democracy by largely undemocratic means has backfired. The attempt to turn the peoples of Europe into Europeans through a common currency, common citizenship and freedom of movement has resulted, paradoxically, in strengthening the forces of extreme nationalism. The attempt to weaken German influence in Europe and the wider world by integrating it more firmly into a radically transformed EU has significantly increased economic and political imbalances, unwittingly empowering Germany vis-à-vis its European partners. Just as Germany has become more European, Europe has been forced, for better or for worse, to become more German. If the twentieth century was plagued by the 'German question' and the violent conflicts that ensued as a result, the twenty-first century is going to be shaped by the 'European question', when Europe at large can no longer be certain of its own destiny. For the European dream *not* to turn into a European nightmare, Europeans need to wake up to a reality that highlights the limits of their own power both at home and abroad.

Politicians and political writers are faced with an impossible task: they cannot predict the future and yet they have to think about ways to improve the current predicament. What went wrong is easier to identify than to fix. However, it is only possible to identify a viable solution for existing problems on the basis of a realistic assessment of the past. This appears to be a major challenge for European elites who, as a result of their dogmatic commitment to an ever-closer union, refuse to acknowledge past mistakes. Europe worked reasonably well up to 1989 because its ambitions were moderated by the awareness of its limits—paradoxically, a supranational project 'rescued' the nation-states of Europe. The effort undertaken after 1989 to substitute a United States of Europe for a Europe of nation-states is destroying democracy at the national level without creating a viable alternative at the European level.

Towards the end of 2011, there are two conflicting scenarios that might rescue Europe from its crisis. One is simply to continue towards an ever-closer union by moving sovereignty more decisively toward a supranational level. This is the option advocated in France and Germany, the two core countries that agreed to create an 'economic government' for Europe. The aim is clearly to subject member states to more external control. This is also advocated by many economic commentators and favoured by the financial markets. However, the people of Europe are at best sceptical, at worst hostile. Greek, Portuguese or Irish voters are not keen to see even more national sovereignty lost to outside forces, whether to the Brussels bureaucracy or the ruling elites in the core member states. At the end of this path would be a Europe with a unified taxation system and shared financing of national budgets achieved through Eurobonds, highly contentious at the time of writing. Such a Europe, however, would also necessitate the abrogation of control over budgets by national parliaments. This scenario would impose an unsustainable financial burden on Germany and an intolerable political burden on the rest of Europe. Budgetary discipline will no longer be enforced by the anonymous markets but by high-profile politicians in Germany and France, alongside faceless bureaucrats in Berlin, Paris and Brussels and the ECB in Frankfurt.

A more likely option, that people in individual member states might force their politicians to reclaim national sovereignty, is not even seriously considered. This would include, in at least some countries of the Eurozone, the re-introduction of the national currency. Pursued in an orderly and managed way, this is almost certainly the best option. Though it is unlikely ever to find the courage, Germany would do a better service to Europe by pursuing its national interest and managing an orderly exit from the Eurozone. This would allow other countries to follow, reclaiming fundamental prerequisites for democracy to work at the national level, such as control over budgetary decisions and priorities. But there can be no doubt that *both* scenarios would be extremely costly and messy.

To deliver more, the EU needs to do less but to do it better. To succeed, Europe must accept the limitations of its post-democratic and post-national politics. Reversing some of the more ambitious EU agendas might be at least as difficult and painful as continuing on the path towards ever-closer union. However, if the continuing march forward causes more harm than good, partial and well-managed disintegration may well be preferable to a chaotic implosion.

What tragic irony: the unravelling of the European project can be dated back to 1989, when Communism collapsed in the East but not owing to pernicious legacies of Communism there—as many people feared might be the case—but, rather, owing to the excessive confidence in the West regarding the possibility of a radically new beginning for Europe as a whole! Europe is failing and has no need for radically new beginnings and further experiments with supranational democracy. It must accept its limitations. It could do worse than learn from a great Irish European, Samuel Beckett, writing in English and French about the perennial problem of our fragile predicament: 'Fail, fail again, fail better.'

Notes

1 Milan Kundera, *The Art of the Novel* (Linda Asher trans.) (New York: Harper Perennial, 2003), p. 129.

2 See Jeremy Rifkin, *The European Dream: How Europe's Vision of the Future is Quietly Eclipsing the American Dream* (Cambridge: Polity, 2004).

3 See Mark Leonard, *Why Europe Will Run the 21st Century* (London: Fourth Estate, 2005).

4 Stephen Hill, *Europe's Promise: Why the European Way is the Best Hope in an Insecure Age* (Berkeley: University of California Press, 2010), p. 18.

5 See Hans Magnus Enzensberger, *Brussels, the Gentle Monster: Or the Disenfranchisement of Europe* (Martin Chalmers trans.) (London,

New York and Calcutta: Seagull Books, 2011), p. 59.

6 Roger Scruton, *The Uses of Pessimism and the Danger of False Hope* (London: Atlantic Books, 2010), p. 102.

7 Paul Valéry, *Variety* (Malcolm Cowley trans.) (San Diego, CA: Harcourt, Brace & Company, 1927), p. 27.

8 Hans Magnus Enzensberger, *Civil War* (Pierce Spence and Martin Chalmers trans) (London: Penguin, 1994), p. 80.

9 Leszek Kołakowski, 'Can Europe Happen?', *New Criterion* 21(9) (May 2003): 19–27. Here, p. 25.

10 Hugo's famous plea for a United States of Europe was a distinctly French attempt to reclaim territories lost in the Franco-Prussian War: 'We shall see France rise again, we shall see her retrieve Lorraine, take back Alsace. But will that be all? No [. . .] seize Trier, Mainz, Cologne, Koblenz, the whole of the left bank of the Rhine.

And we shall hear France cry out: It's my turn, Germany, here I am! Am I your enemy? No! I am your sister. I have taken back everything and I give you everything, on one condition: that we shall act as one people, as one family, as one Republic [. . .] My revenge is fraternity! No more frontiers!' Cited in David Marsh, *The Euro: The Politics of the New Global Currency* (New Haven, CT: Yale University Press, 2009), p. 21.

11 Heinrich Schenker, *Beethoven's Ninth Symphony* (J. Rothgeb trans.) (New Haven: Yale University Press, 1992), p. 234.

12 Tony Judt, *A Grand Illusion?: An Essay on Europe* (New York: Hill and Wang, 1996), p. 43.

13 See Alan S. Milward, *The European Rescue of the Nation-State* (London: Routledge, 1992).

14 One of the best videos about the 2004 EU enlargement is devoted to Bulgaria's accession: 'Bulgaria in EU: Ode to Joy', produced by the European Commission Audiovisual Services. It is also underlined

by Beethoven's Ninth Symphony. Available at: http://www.youtube.com/watch?v=5YR-ATIjKU

15 Judt, *A Grand Illusion?*, p. 14.

16 Franz C. Mayer and Jan Palmowski, 'European Identities and the EU: The Ties that Bind the Peoples of Europe', *Journal of Common Market Studies* 42(3) (September 2004): 573–98. Here, p. 580.

17 This slogan usually entails, particularly in Germany, the rejection of the ultimate crime of the Second World War: 'never again Auschwitz'. The Holocaust can thus be viewed as the EU's foundational myth. The nations in Central and Eastern Europe have sought to expand on this narrative by including the rejection of Stalinism alongside Nazism in the European self-understanding. This cause has been advanced in the European Parliament which, in September 2008, designated 23 August —the anniversary of the Nazi–Soviet non-aggression pact of 1939—as the 'European

Day of Remembrance for Victims of Stalinism and Nazism'.

18 It is worthwhile noting that the anthem does this implicitly, for it has no lyrics—it is 'truly a bastard child of the Enlightenment: a song without words; hope without a text'. See Caryl Clark, 'Forging Identity: Beethoven's "Ode" as European Anthem', *Critical Inquiry* 23(4) (Summer 1997): 789–807. Here, p. 801. Yet, Clark's detailed study also shows why this was politically necessary: 'to sanction a German-language text would risk disturbing the ghost that still haunts the European Union—the ghost of Germany ascendant' (p. 803). Moreover, the ratification of the Lisbon Treaty in November 2009 further reduced the official status of the anthem; there is no explicit reference to it as envisaged by the failed Constitutional Treaty. Thus, the EU has an anthem without words that dares not speak its name.

19 Esteban Buch, 'Beethoven in the Shadows of Berlin: Karajan's European Anthem', *Dissent* 56(4) (Fall 2009): 14–17. Here, p. 17.

20 Very few serious commentators might be as blinded by their enthusiasm for the EU as to consider it the main reason for the demise of Communism. Yet William Pfaff, for one, celebrated the fiftieth anniversary of the Treaty of Rome by proclaiming: 'Fundamentally, the EU did it [. . .] The European Union, more than any other single factor, was responsible for the defeat of the Soviet Union in the cold war.' See William Pfaff, 'Happy Birthday!', *New York Review of Books* 54(7) (26 April 2007–9 May 2007): 20.

21 The video is available at http://www.youtube.com/watch?v=nhS55x8J7pw

22 This production may well have satisfied most Polish viewers (as can be seen from their responses on the YouTube page), but it found generally far less viewers than the original video to which it responded. More

information about the video and a web link are available at: http://wyborcza.pl/1,76842,-6688700,UE_poprawila_spot_i_dodala_Bono__zobacz_film_.html

23 Roszkowski proclaimed the publication 'a failure', concluding, 'The intention of creating common French–German memory in the young generation has become all the world to the authors. Since [. . .] European integration takes so much space then, why is there no information about problems of Ireland, Sweden, Finland, Denmark, Italy, Portugal, Greece or Cyprus, not to mention Eastern and Central European countries? The knowledge from the textbook will shape the student's incorrect belief that overcoming German and French nationalisms has enabled Europe to solve its main problems and that these two countries are supposed to play a special role in Europe and their mission is to manage the affairs of the European Union and European

historical memory.' See http://www.euroclio.eu/download/2009/Wojciech%20Roszkowski%20%20Criticism%20of%20New%20History%20Textbook.pdf

24 The letter addressed to the president of the European Parliament on 4 December 2008 listed 22 objections against the 'Conceptual Basis for a House of European History' and was signed by 13 MEPs starting with Adam Bielan and Wojciech Roszkowski—both from the Polish conservative Law and Justice Party (Prawo i Sprawiedliwość), which became a crucial partner for the UK Tories in creating a new antifederalist group, the European Conservatives and Reformists—and finishing with György Schöpflin, a distinguished political scientist from Hungary's conservative Fidesz party, which is a member of the Group of the European People's Party. See http://www.roszkowski.pl/www/-media/files/-aktualnosci/2008/34/List_ws_Domu_Historii.pdf

25 Claus Leggewie, *Der Kampf um die europäische Erinnerung* (The Struggle for European Memory) (Munich: C. H. Beck, 2011), pp. 182–3.

26 Adam Krzemiński, 'Der Kniefall' in *Deutsche Erinnerungsorte I* (German Memorial Places) (Hagen Schulze and Etienne Francois eds) (Munich: C. H. Beck, 2001), p. 441.

27 Johann George Reißmüller, 'Deutsche Verhältnisse' (German Circumstances), *Frankfurter Allgemeine Zeitung* (14 December 1981), p. 1.

28 Rudolf Augstein, 'Die Polnische Tragödie' (The Polish Tragedy), *Der Spiegel* 35(52) (21 December 1981): 88.

29 'Für Brandt kein Thema' (No Issue for Brandt), *Frankfurter Allgemeine Zeitung* (22 December 1981), p. 10.

30 Václav Havel, 'Anatomy of a Reticence' (Erazim Kohák trans.) in *Open Letters: Selected Writings, 1965–1990* (Paul Wilson ed.) (New York: Vintage, 1992).

31 'Einigkeit und Recht und Freiheit für das deutsche Vaterland' (Unity and Justice and Freedom for the German Fatherland). (Footage available in the archive of the German TV, ZDF at: http://www.zdf.de/ZDF-mediathek/beitrag/video/351164/Bundestag-singt-am-9.11.1989) Although the anthem was intoned by a handful of MPs from the conservative Christian Democratic and Christian Social Union (Herman J. Unland, Franz Sauter and Ernst Hinsken), all MPs from both right-wing and left-wing political parties joined in.

32 Helmut Kohl, *Erinnerungen, 1982–1990* (Memories, 1982–1990) (Munich: Droemer, 2005), p. 967.

33 Hans-Dietrich Genscher, the then German foreign minister, has described how the ambivalent attitude of the Polish people was reflected by the Polish leadership. During a working breakfast on 10 November 1989, he observed that 'Lech Wałęsa was worried, if not shocked about the demise

of the Wall', while Bronisław Geremek, noticing Genscher's consternation at Wałęsa's reaction, assured him that the 'development was delightful for Germans and Europe, as well as Poland.' Cited in Hans-Dietrich Genscher, *Erinnerungen* (Memories) (Berlin: Siedler Verlag, 1995), p. 655.

34 Zespół problemowy polskiego porozumienia niepodległościowego (Polish Alliance for Independence), 'Niemcy a Polska' (Germany and Poland), *Kultura* 7 (July–August 1978): 123–9. Here p. 127.

35 Cited in George Jones, 'Polish PM Adopts WW2 Rhetoric in EU Summit', *Telegraph* (21 June 2007). Available at: http://www.telegraph.co.uk/news/uknews/1555189/Polish-PM-adopts-WW2-rhetoric-at-EU-summit.html

36 Gerhard Schröder, 'Ohne polnisches Freiheitsstreben wäre die Geschichte der deutschen Einheit weniger glücklich verlaufen' (The History of German Unification Would Have Been Less Fortunate without the Polish Fight for Freedom),

Frankfurter Allgemeine Zeitung (7 December 2000), p. 10.

37 Ivan Krastev, '"Epoka przebaczenia" versus "epoka normalności"' ('The Era of Forgiveness' versus 'the Normal Age'), introduction to K. Wigura (ed.), *Wina narodów* (Warsaw: Wydawnictwo Naukowe Scholar, 2011), pp. 7–12. Here, p. 8.

38 Joschka Fischer, interviewed by the author. 4 July 2011, Berlin. Available at: http://-itunes.apple.com/au/itunes-u/-european-union-studies/id392882228

39 See Jürgen Habermas, *Postnational Constellations* (Max Pensky ed. and trans.) (Cambridge, MA: MIT Press, 2001).

40 See Ulrich Beck and Edgar Grande, *Cosmopolitan Europe* (Ciaran Cronin trans.) (Cambridge: Polity, 2007).

41 Beck, 'Mein Gott, was für eine Chance!' (My God, What an Opportunity!), *Die Zeit* (19 March 2009), p. 11; 'This Economic Crisis Cries Out to be Transformed into the

Founding of a New Europe', *Guardian* (13 April 2009). Available at: http://www.guardian.co.uk/commentisfr-ee/2009/apr/13/european-union-economic-crisis

Similar versions of this article appeared in a number of European languages but, while German, Czech, Polish and Slovak versions all describe the 2009 crisis as the 'second world revolution', the English rendition omits this.

42 This used to be the domain of British tabloid newspapers, which received new feeding ground for stories with every new step towards closer integration of the Eurozone. After a Franco-German summit that proposed a EU economic government, Simon Heffer commented: 'Where Hitler failed by military means to conquer Europe, modern Germans are succeeding through trade and financial discipline. Welcome to the Fourth Reich.' See Simon Heffer, 'Rise of the Fourth Reich, How Germany is Using the Financial Crisis to Conquer Europe',

Daily Mail (17 August 2011). Available at: http://www.dailymail.co.uk/news/article-2026840/European-debt-summit-Germany-using-financial-crisis-conquer-Europe.html

43 Cited in Ulrike Guérot and Mark Leonard, 'The New German Question: How Europe Can Get the Germany it Needs', *European Council on Foreign Relations Policy Brief* 30 (April 2011): 7. Available at: http://www.ecfr.eu/page//ECFR30_GERMANY_AW.pdf

44 Cited in Konrad Putzier, 'Das vierte Reich—Deutschland erobert Europa' (The Fourth Reich—Germany Conquers Europe), *Die Welt* (19 August, 2011).

45 Dostoyevsky's gambler was refreshingly honest about his disdain for such qualities: 'To the German method of heaping up riches [. . .] I can tell you that what I have seen and verified makes my Tartar blood boil. Good Lord! I wish for no virtues of that kind [. . .] I found that things were even as we read of them in good German

picture-books—that every house has its "Fater", who is horribly beneficent and extraordinarily honourable. So honourable is he that it is dreadful to have anything to do with him; and I cannot bear people of that sort.' See Fyodor Dostoyevsky, *The Gambler* (C. J. Hogarth trans.) (Montana: Kessinger Publishing, 2004), p. 23.

46 Cited in Mara Delius, 'Die Deutschen nerven mit ihrer Rechthaberei' (Germans Annoy Me with Their Know-It-All Attitude), *Die Welt* (27 October 2010). Available at: http://www.-welt.de/print/die_welt/kultur/article-10561175/Die-Deutschen-nerven-mit-ihrer-Rechthaberei.html

47 Leon de Winter, 'Zurück zur EWG' (Back to the EEC), *Der Spiegel* 64(20) (2010): 150–2. Here, p. 151.

48 This is reflected in an opinion survey from July 2011, which suggested that far fewer Germans consider France and other European nations as their vital allies than was the case less than a decade ago. In

contrast, the perceived importance of China and Russia has increased. See Dieter Frankenberger, 'Zu neuen Ufern? In Deutschland verändern sich die außenpolitischen Mentalitäten' (New Pastures? Change in Germany's Foreign Policy Attitudes), *Frankfurter Allgemeine Zeitung* (21 July 2011), p. 3.

49 Andrew Rettman, 'Brussels Rebukes Slovakia over Greek U-turn', *euobserver.com* (12 August 2010). Available at: http://euobserver.com/19/30610

50 See Richard Sulik, 'Richarda Sulíka na tému euroval v NR SR' (Speech by Richard Sulik on Euroval in Parliament). Available at: http://www.strana-sas.sk/rec-richarda-sulika-na-temu-euroval-v-nr-sr/430

51 Kalypso Nicolaïdis, 'The Struggle for EUrope', *Dissent* 52(4) (Fall 2005): 11–17. Here, p. 16–17.

52 Kalypso Nicolaïdis, 'We the Peoples of Europe: A More Perfect Union', *Foreign Affairs* 83(6) (2004): 97–110. Here, p. 103.

53 'Juncker: "Die Souveränität der Griechen wird eingeschränkt"'(Juncker: 'The Sovereignty of the Greeks is Reduced'), *Focus* (3 July 2011). Available at: http://www.focus.de/finanzen/news/staatsverschuldung/juncker-die-souveraenitaet-der-griechen-wird-eingeschraenkt_aid_642496.html

The argument was echoed by German Finance Minister Wolfgang Schäuble a few weeks later. See 'EU-Problemstaaten müssen für Hilfen Hoheitsrechte abgeben' (EU Countries Must Sacrifice their Sovereignty for Assistance), *Stern* (28 July 2011). Available at: http://www.stern.de/news2/aktuell/-eu-problemstaaten-muessen-fuer-hilfen-hoheitsrechte-abgeben-1710633.html

54 David Marsh, 'Faltering Ambitions and Unrequited Hopes: The Battle for the Euro Intensifies', *Journal of Common Market Studies* 49 (Annual Review) (2011): 45–55. Here, p. 49.

55 Ibid., p. 51.

56 Ibid., p. 54.

Further reading

BUTI, Marco, Servaas Deroose, Vitor Gaspar and Joao Nogueira Martins (eds). *The Euro: The First Decade*. Cambridge: Cambridge University Press, 2010.

HABERMAS, Jürgen. 'Wir brauchen Europa!' (We Need Europe!). *Die Zeit*, 20 May 2010, p. 47.

——. 'Merkels von Demoskopie geleiteter Opportunismus' (Merkel Guided by Opinion Polls Opportunism). *Süddeutsche Zeitung*, 7 April 2011. Available at http://www.sueddeutsche.de/politik/europapolitik-merkels-von-demoskopie-geleiteter-opportunismus-1.1082536

JUDT, Tony. *Postwar: A History of Europe since 1945*. London: William Heinemann, 2005.

Lyons, Carole. 'A Door into the Dark; Doing Justice to History in the Courts of the European Union'. *EUI Working Papers Law* 11:1–91. Florence: European University Institute, 2008. Avaialble at: http://cadmus.-eui.eu/bitstream/handle-/1814/8308/LAW-2-008-11.pdf-?sequence=1

Mercier, Paul and F. Papadia. *The Concrete Euro: Implementing Monetary Policy in the Euro Area*. Oxford: Oxford University Press, 2011.